A to Z of
Helping
Hands

Tracy Nelson Maurer

Rourke Publishing LLC
Vero Beach, Florida 32964

About The Author:

Tracy Nelson Maurer specializes in nonfiction and business writing. Her most recently published children's books include the Green Thumb Guides series, also from the Rourke Book Company. A University of Minnesota graduate, Tracy lives with her husband Mike and two children in Superior, Wisconsin.

Acknowledgments:

With appreciation to Margaret and Thomas for their joyful assistance in developing this series, and to Lois M. Nelson for her editing and enthusiastic support.

PHOTO CREDITS:
© Photodisc, cover; © Linda Dingman, page 4, 6, 12, 16, 30, 44, 46; © Diane Farleo, page 24, 26, 36, 37, 38; © Julie Johanik, page 13, 18, 22, 25, 28, 40, 42; © Lois M. Nelson, page 8, 10, 14, 20, 32, 34

Library of Congress Cataloging-in-Publication Data

Maurer, Tracy, 1965–
   A to Z of helping hands / Tracy Nelson Maurer.
      p. cm. — (A to Z)
   ISBN 1-58952-061-0
   1. Work—Juvenile literature. 2. Helping behavior—Juvenile literature. 3. Thoughtfulness—Juvenile literature. [1. Helpfulness. 2. Thoughtfulness. 3. Alphabet.] I. Title

HQ784.W6 M38 2001
306.3'6 E—dc21

                                                                                    2001018587

Printed in the USA

Little Hands, Big Helpers

Helping hands come in all sizes. Your hands are just the right size to help around your house and at school. Friends, family, teachers and even people you don't know will like the nice things you can do. Try these ideas from A to Z, and you'll think of many more ways to put your helping hands to work!

5

Answer the telephone nicely.

Aa

Bounce your ball outside.

Bb

NOPQRSTUVWXYZ

A B C D E F G H I J K L M

Cc

Clear the windows.

ABCDEFGHIJKLM

Dig weeds in the garden.

Dd

Empty the cup when you finish.

Ee

A B C D E F G H I J K L M

Feed the fish.

Ff

NOPQRSTUVWXYZ

A B C D E F G H I J K L M

Guard the school crossing.

Gg

ABCDEFGHIJKLM

Hh

Hang up your coat.

A B C D E F G H I J K L M

Include your sister in the fun.

NOPQRSTUVWXYZ

ABCDEFGHIJKLM

Jump out of the way.

Jj

NOPQRSTUVWXYZ

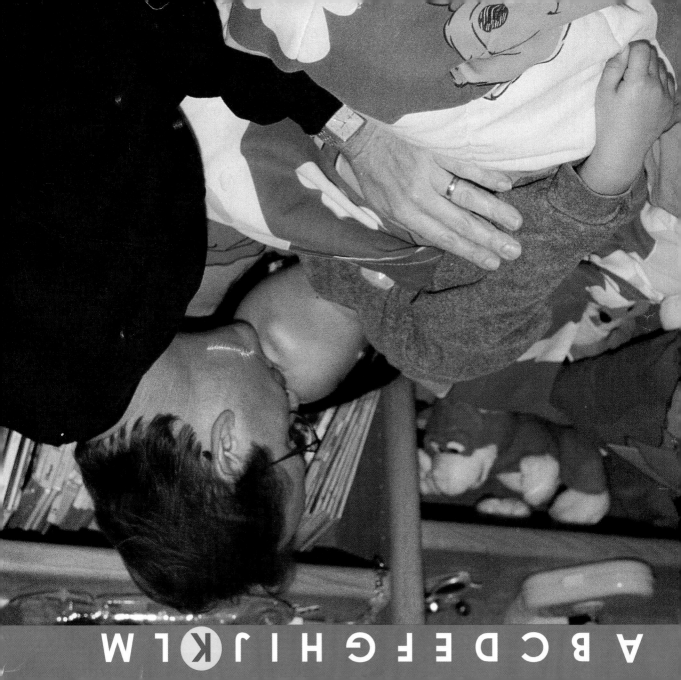

ABCDEFGHIJKLM

Kiss good night.

NOPQRSTUVWXYZ

Ll

Load the dishwasher.

24

Mm

Make your bed.

Neaten the books.

Nn

A B C D E F G H I J K L M

Offer an apple.

Oo

A B C D E F G H I J K L M

Put your toys away.

Pp

NOPQRSTUVWXYZ

Quit running by the pool.

ABCDEFGHIJKLM

Rake the leaves.

Rr

Set the table.

Ss

ABCDEFGHIJKLM

Take out the trash.

41

ABCDEFGHIJKLM

Unload the groceries.

Uu

ABCDEFGHIJKLM

Vv

Vacuum the carpet.

ABCDEFGHIJKLM

Wash the dishes.

Ww

N O P Q R S T U V W X Y Z

ABCDEFGHIJKLM

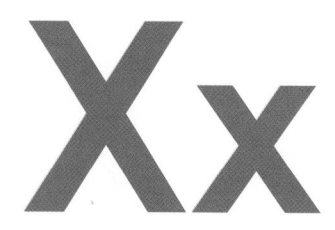

Exit in a neat line.

ABCDEFGHIJKLM

Yy

Yell outside, not inside.

47

NOPQRSTUVWXYZ

Zz

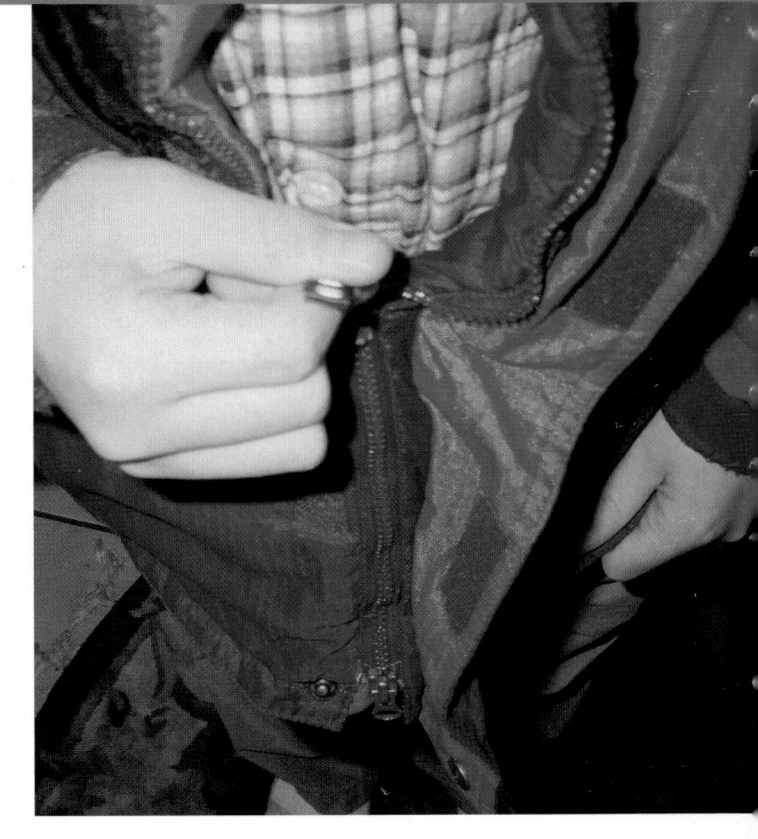

Zip up your zipper.

48